Southern Messenger Poets

DAVE SMITH, EDITOR

Also by David Huddle

POETRY

Paper Boy
Stopping by Home
The Nature of Yearning
Summer Lake: New & Selected Poems

FICTION

A Dream With No Stump Roots In It
Only The Little Bone
The High Spirits: Stories of Men and Women
Intimates
Tenorman
The Story of a Million Years
Not: A Trio—A Novella and Two Stories
La Tour Dreams of the Wolf Girl

NONFICTION

The Writing Habit

POETRY, FICTION, AND NONFICTION

A David Huddle Reader

Grayscale

David Huddle

poems

LOUISIANA STATE UNIVERSITY PRESS
BATON ROUGE
2004

Designer: Melanie O'Quinn Samaha
Typeface: Minion
Printer and binder: Thomson-Shore, Inc.

Library of Congress Cataloging-in-Publication Data

Huddle, David, 1942–
    Grayscale : poems / David Huddle.
        p. cm.
    ISBN 0-8071-2949-6 (cloth : alk. paper) — ISBN 0-8071-2950-X (pbk. :
alk. paper)
    I. Title.
    PS3558.U287G73 2004
    811'.54—dc22

                                                                    2003017758

The paper in this book meets the guidelines
for permanence and durability of the Committee on
Production Guidelines for Book Longevity of the
Council on Library Resources. ∞

The author offers grateful acknowledgment to the editors of the following pub-
lications, in which some of the poems herein originally appeared, sometimes
in a different form: *American Literary Review:* "The Poem, the Snow, Jane
Goodall, the Vase of Daffodils"; *Cortland Review:* "April Saturday"; *Green
Mountains Review:* "The Penguin Sonatas"; *Hampden-Sydney Poetry Review:*
"Anything Goes"; *Hollins Critic:* "Crossing New River"; *5 AM:* "Natural
Pedagogy"; *Rivendell:* "Myself in Retrospect," "Deathlight"; *Seneca Review:*
"Circus"; *Witness:* "Remarkable Birdsong in Denton, Texas."

for George Garrett

Contents

Three Generations
of Blue Ridge Mountain Women
Speak Across Time

for Molly Huddle
at William & Mary
on the occasion
of her eighteenth birthday—
October 14, 2000

Our faces must tell you our lives
aren't easy—but difficulty lives
in every heart. Look at our hands,
our hair, our collars, these hand-
sewn hems of our skirts. Daisies
came each summer to ease our days.
There is only this single picture
of us. No writer ever picked our
stories for a book. We had dreams
of you, so we send you this dream
of us from the past: three women
who choose flowers for their omen.

Stiffly posed before the forsythia bush, they wear
coats, ties, and bemused faces, as if their mother's
just called to them from the porch, "You boys
hold your shoulders back and stand up straight."

Here is where they played three thousand
croquet games, some that lasted well beyond
twilight and on into such summer darkness
as arouses a yard full of lightning bugs.

No mallets or wickets are visible here—
this day looks to be a solemn occasion.
These young men are becoming acquainted
with time's optical illusion: we think

we stand in the vivid color of here and now
and view the past as drab black and white,
whereas the truth is—it's our future
that's the off-center, badly-focused grayscale,

the day coming when someone picks up
a snapshot and says, just before
tossing it to oblivion, "My god,
who are these quaint people?"

Charles Richard Huddle, III, named
for his father and grandfather;
William Royal Huddle, named
for Uncle Bill from California;

and David Ross Huddle, named
for great-grandmother Katherine Ross,
whose face he never saw. These names I write
on a morning of blowing snow in Vermont.

Change

In the hall closet
(where there was no light)
in the shoe-box size
Chinese wooden box
that could be opened
only through the five
steps of a puzzle,
with my father's coin
collection that had
in it money from
all over the world,
was the special jar—
glass tube exactly
the right size to hold
twenty-five silver
dollars, one for each
year since 1912,
the year he was born,
some easy for him
to find, others so
difficult they were
too expensive
to buy in the year
I did what I did—
1948.

The weight of that jar,
the slight clink it made
when I tilted it—
what made me take it
I can't exactly say
but can still somehow
feel in my body.

Some of the dollars
I used to buy goods
for the grocery
stand I intended
to set up behind
our garage—Grapette

and Ritz Crackers.
Some I slipped to friends
of my big brother
to make them like me
more than him. About
half the jar was gone
by the time they caught
me, the six year old thief turned businessman
and politician.
The crime was too grave
for a spanking—I got
such a serious
talking to I'd rather
have had the hairbrush.
My father made no
effort to replace
the dollars—he'd stopped
collecting coins
many years ago—
and it soon wasn't
mentioned any more.
My childhood went back
to normal except
for the way I'd see
my father sometimes
sort of studying me.

1955

On single staved sheets, each part
in a different colored ink, my father
had copied out arrangements of songs
like "The Little Brown Church in the Dale,"

"Jeannie with the Light Brown Hair," and "I Want
a Girl Just Like the Girl." That summer,
when the two of us sat side by side,
my sax and his trumpet sounded half decent.

Thirteen, just learning how to play, I
had my pants pegged, my hair slicked back,
a pack of cigarettes hidden in the garage,
and a girl whose phone number I'd memorized, but

after supper, for a few weeks, my father had me
sit down with him and make old-time harmony.

Inheritance

I have this from Grandmama Huddle: I want
my coffee so hot I can barely sip it,
but I also like it with plenty of milk.
Like her, I heat my cup with boiling water—

a trick that works well enough through the first third
of the cup, but then it cools as God decrees
it must, and that's when I remember her gaze
out her kitchen window to the sprawl of out-

buildings, broken-down orchard, and scrub pasture
that were what her life had come to when she was
sixty-five and I was fifteen, and we were
more or less chatting as she ate her breakfast.

I wondered then—but don't any more—what she saw
out there that made her look the way she did.

Natural Pedagogy

Aunt Murrell got L. J.
to hook a hot wire
to the bird feeder
so that whenever a squirrel

climbed up there she could flip
a switch beside her kitchen window
and shoot just enough
juice into the squirrel

to knock it off
the feeder, thereby teaching
it a basic difference
between birds and squirrels—

the former were welcome
to eat at her feeder,
the latter should look elsewhere.
I watched her educate a squirrel

once—that thing gyrated
into the air and hit the grass
running. Aunt Murrell's face
expressed sympathy for her pupil,

of course, but there was pleasure,
too, appropriate for a teacher
who'd found a sure-fire method
of improving squirrels.

Myself in Retrospect

Last night as I was making what I thought
was a funny dinner-table remark,
it happened again—I imagined Lindsey
and Molly recalling what I'd just said
years after my death: *Do you remember
that time Dad . . .* You'd think such an idea
would be disturbing, but not so. An odd
comfort came with it: *Even when I'm dead,
we can still clown around at dinnertime.*
I don't even mind how I enter this
dimension more and more often—live me
and dead me reading through the old contract,
going over the fine print to make sure
I understand the terms of my release.

Return of the Dinosaurs

for Bess

I'd set your dinosaurs against
your Barbies, the Brontosaurus mouth
just right to grasp a dainty foot.

That orange fin-backed one loved you
to come shrieking to save Disco,
California, or Rock Star.

And when Tyrannosaurus Rex
galloped away with Ballerina's
make-up kit and you wept the real tears

that should have made me give it up,
I said, "Them boys agonna chew
awhile on Prom Night Barbie's arm."

One morning I looked for my girl-
tormentors but they had vanished.
I used all my tricks, searched the house

like a detective, nearly begged
and even almost ordered you
to give them back, but they never

turned up. History does its trick:
your sister came along, you both
grew up, and we banished your toys—

carried them down to the basement,
one by one, to become antiques.
Your mother and I are trying

to learn our lesson, how to live
without daughters around to tease.
You never revealed your secret

hiding place, and you don't have to
explain why this last visit home you
remembered them boys and set them

out on my writing table—old

Orange F.B., Brontosaurus,
and mighty Tyrannosaurus Rex,

blinking under my halogen
lamp, making their necessary
adjustments to a whole new world.

Public Place

When Melva was thirteen
her mother
didn't want her
wearing shorts downtown.

Fifteen years old
and her boyfriend,
I helped her sneak
to do it. I don't know why

Melva and I thought downtown
needed to see her
in those white shorts
with the little ties at each hip.

She and I went to the Wythe Theatre,
where, in the cool dark,
we kissed, we put our hands
on each other, and

of course somebody
called in a report
to Melva's mother, a friend
of my own mother, and a dear woman

who on that sunny afternoon
deserved better
from Melva
and me, too, I guess.

Cancer took Mrs. Stephens
and later Melva,
and eventually even most
of downtown Wytheville, Virginia,

which must have something to do
with why I think you living
strangers need to know about that day
of long-ago tawdry glory.

I'd seen two fifth-grade friends pulled up by hooks
and flopped into rescue squad boats—blue shirts,
dark jeans, heavy high-top shoes streaming mud-
darkened water.
          And if I remember
that so clearly after forty-eight years—
and if I've never been a strong swimmer,
always been fearful of water,
                then why
did I—even just this once!—choose to swim
across with Eddie Wolcott, my high school
pal? (He's long dead now, natural causes,
of course.)
          Well, I don't think there's an answer
to that question. I could say it was dog
days weather, school would start in a couple
of weeks, Eddie and I were bored, downstream
toward Austinville, no one else around,
the fish totally uninterested
in what we had to offer, and the water—
that old coffee and cream living creature
of a New River, steadily flowing north
—got us in the trance of watching its swirls
and ripples.
          That's when Eddie asked, "Want to?"
and I said, "No." Then he said, "Oh come on,"
and so I did. The two of us stripped down,
waded out, and swam across. Harder was
getting back. The current had carried us
downstream, and so, naked as savages,
we had to walk the rocky bank upstream
half a mile or so to aim ourselves back
down to our clothes and fishing gear.
                I must
have been tired that day, and probably glad
to be alive, but I'm only guessing.
What I do remember is how strange it felt
to be naked on the far bank, scraping
bare feet, shins, and ankles on the mean rocks

over there, and how we talked as we made
our tedious way—muddy to the knees—
about how really cool it would be if
Velma Williams and Bonnie Demers were there
with us, bare-ass naked—as we'd never
seen them—on the other side of the world.

April Saturday, 1960

I mean, Berkley Osborne and I had
small interest in each other, and

it was happenstance the afternoon
we found ourselves in the ballroom

of Wytheville Country Club, nobody
else around except Judy and Bobby,

her cousin and my pal, so serious
a couple they lost interest in us

immediately, put on a slow record
and stepped out on the dance floor

to do something that could hardly
be called a dance. An undulating

embrace was what it was. Berkley
and I—joking—started a mannerly

box step. We'd spoken hardly ten
sentences before—maybe I grinned

at her one day in the hall or she
at me in band practice or history

but we'd never touched fingertips
let alone tried to dance. So it's

no wonder we began in awkwardness
and humor, poking fun at the kiss

Bobby and Judy showed no signs of
breaking off. It's strange enough

two couples dancing in a ballroom
with all the invisible chaperones

tsk-tsking, the other dancers not
yet having arrived, full daylight

reflecting over the parquet floor,
a line of chairs for wallflowers

along three walls, tables whitely
waiting for punch bowls perfectly

centered among cups, small plates
for cookies, party napkins placed

exactly so. Music stands awaited
sax man, trumpeter and trombonist;

the discreet piano widely grinned,
and the drums and cymbals yearned

to be punished. Meanwhile Berkley
and I box-stepped our laps nicely

around the ballroom. "Oh my God!"
whispered Berkley; she gave a nod

toward Bobby and Judy, only their
pelvises moving, his hands on her

butt and hers on his. They stood
in place, clothes on, a very good

boy and girl except for movements
of their tongues, hips, and hands.

The record that kept on repeating
was the soulful "Unchained Melody"

which cast a spell over the whole
room—it was like a space capsule

floating endlessly toward unknown
galaxies of eternal mid-afternoon

light with Berkley and me in orbit
around a red-hot Bobby-Judy planet.

Well, the box step grows tiresome
after you step out box number one

thousand and four. Berkley and I
shifted position, she gave a sigh

then snuggled in close. I noticed
her warmth and her nice fragrance,

also her astoundingly small waist,
and the way her chest fit against

my chest. I think that's actually
what caused the glandular anomaly

that followed—we sort of scooted
our chests around as if we needed

to get comfortable, the sensation
being about as erotic as anything

I've ever felt. So Berkley and I
were acquaintances transmogrified

suddenly into your basic two part
hormonally effervescent lust-unit.

One minute we were innocently box-
stepping away our lives, the next

we were groins and nipples, pubic
hair, teeth and tongues, a public

display of live pornography—well,
I shouldn't exaggerate. We still

had our clothes on, and we didn't
collapse to the floor. The event

was so mental and over so quickly
that the annals of sexual history

don't even mention it. All right,
maybe it was no more than a tight

embrace with a remarkably intense
kiss and maybe the body movements

of accomplished lovers like Bobby
and Judy. Maybe a favorite hobby

of theirs was leading mere casual
friends into situations of carnal

possibility—Berkley and I locked
into each other, parts of a clock

fitting perfectly, moving in time.
We were just kids really, sixteen

and seventeen, we hadn't had much
experience, certainly not of such

intensity or strangeness. I think
Eros looked at Cupid, gave a wink,

and suddenly Berkley sighed, "O,"
which took me over the edge. "O,"

I said, too. We just stood there
breathing and shuddering together.

Embarrassment set in very quickly,
but it was of the bonding variety,

and of course we couldn't go back
to the box step. We tried to chat

and stand where we were, our arms
still around each other, our aims

a bit vague and sentimental. How
kind words were to come to us now

that we had learned such a lesson
of recapitulating ontology, human

folly, and the utter indifference
of stars drifting through silence.

"I have to go to tuck my shirt in"
or "I should splash cold water on

my face" or "Shouldn't we get out
of here?"—our exact words aren't

the point. At a certain emotional
pitch, the tone of a voice is all

that matters, *somebody just croon
to me please, and I'll be ok soon.*

Ten thousand days have flown away
since that small piece of a sunny

afternoon. Berkley's had her life,
I've had mine, and who can say if

what happened made any difference
to either of us? Her remembrance

may bring her a twitch of a smile
but that's all. Sometimes I feel

I'm a sliver of dust in the great
pattern of creation, I think fate

is a vast intelligence. But then
I recall blips of cosmic nonsense

like that afternoon with Berkley:
Galactic energy started crackling

along the stratospheric periphery
with Darwin and Freud spastically

heaving in their graves and a boy
and a girl in a Virginia town, by

the whimsy of chaos, the theology
of random chance, were flung body

against body. Bless their hearts,
they played their ludicrous parts,

saying "O," and standing in place,
with astonishing kindness and grace.

Anything Goes

We often speculate about exactly
where anything goes and why.
The coffee's slightly bitter, light
goes thin around the edges, dogs
incessantly sniff our yard, and books
don't cheer us up the way they should.
We don't know why anything
abandons us this way. Still,
if anything means anything,
we know we can't be possessive,
can't always be whining, "Where's
anything, for God's sake? I just
dropped my shoelace down three flights
of stairs, and anything's nowhere
to be found." We try to be strong
in the absence of anything.
"Buck up," we say. "Anything'll
be back soon, and then it'll be
laissez les bon temps roulez."
Comes a sunny day, the chickadees
are playing grabass in the tulip beds,
the car radio gives us three good songs
in a row, a little check comes
in the mail, and that's when we know
anything's back in town. "Let's go
look for anything," we say. "Let's go out
and lasso that sucker. Let's take anything
for a ride in the country, tell jokes,
buy creemees, check in to a motel, make out,
watch old movies on the TV, and drink
cheap beer till we get sick or run out
of money, whichever comes first." This is what
anything always does to us, makes us silly
for no good reason. Which is the point,
really, of anything. Which is also why
we don't mind so much when anything
gives us that old familiar look and says,
"Fuck this," heading for the door.

Pornography in Hell

Locked as we are
  in this fantastic chain
    of flesh—ten billion bodies endlessly
      writhing without love or speech,
        denied even simple affection
          for each other and by now
    afflicted with complete
      revulsion for the human
        body—all

we can do is moan, grunt, twitch,
   and undulate as if it were pleasure
     we sought instead of the impossible
       freedom for which we so incessantly
         yearn. Oh, to be without
            the hateful breast that stuffs
     my mouth, that oafish penis
       forever plunging into my exhausted
         vagina, and these silly

clitorises ceaselessly rubbing
   against my fingertips—Oh, just finally, please, to come
     and be done with myself
       and these wretched others,
         every one of us driven to probe,
           suck, rub, lick, but never to touch
     the peace the body
       promises us. Surely you can see
         why we crave it—and why of course

we even help each other to steal a moment
   every hundred years or so
     to read a single page copied
       from someone's memory of the living
         world where it was despised
           and now, here, passionately
    smuggled from one to another
      of us, hidden in the sweatiest
         crevices, the words sometimes smeared

beyond recognition but even two lines
      can bring tears to one
            of us souls damned
                  eternally to what the living
                        consider ecstasy—I tell you I'll never
                              forget seeing a woman shudder
            as she read, "About suffering they were never . . ."
                and a man who ejaculated
                    (we hadn't ever seen it here)

so copiously that we cheered him
      as he bellowed, "blackberry, blackberry, blackberry,"
            and I, too, am fairly certain
                that I experienced a discreet but definite
                    pleasuring with "Penguin dust,
                        bring me penguin dust." The hope
            of such words once again seething across
                my mind's tongue helps me abide these hands
                  that won't stop stroking my thighs.

Banyan

I'm giving up the idea that my tattoo
will spring forth from inner necessity—
that one morning I'll wake up knowing it
must be a python winding down my thigh,

a blue rose just beneath my right kneecap,
or the Byzantine Christ's face on my back.
I know I've got to choose it, pick it from
the ten billion pictures the universe

has so kindly let pass before my eyes
or rise up in my imagination.
At my age, what difference does it make
to anyone but myself what image

I have needled into my skin? What book
do I want to read, painting do I want
to see, song do I want to hear, woman
do I want to kiss before I check out

of this life? That's the kind of choice it is,
one picture to go down into the cold,
cold ground with me. I'm beginning to see
that it's got to be one of those ancient

trees, not a redwood or sequoia—they
grow too tall—but one that extends outward,
branches horizontal to the ground like wings,
a trunk so thick a whole kindergarten

of kids couldn't link hands around it.
I want its leaves to green up my whole chest,
its trunk to go down my belly and legs,
its roots plummeting through my feet—and birds!

I want birds flying across my shoulders,
my back and arms, egrets, sparrows, condors,
and chickadees, all winging toward rest
in the great tree where I've hidden my body.

Is There Anybody Here I Can Say Goodbye To?

My locker and Ray's locker
are near enough we'd be rude
if we didn't talk—so we do,
couple times a week, polite

exchanges being the limits
of my interest, but Ray being
retired and eager to tell
about his career, including what

the dean told him twenty years ago
and what he told the dean;
Ray being a Republican
and ready to talk politics;

Ray being a snowbird;
which is to say a winter
resident of Florida,
with plenty to say

about the weather there
versus the weather here—
it's real nice there,
whereas here, well, it can

make you shake your head
and give a low whistle;
Ray just plain being
friendly, a cheerful *hey*

for almost everybody
who's got a locker
nearby, students, profs,
custodians, even the cage

guys who sometimes walk
through there; but with Ray
you want to keep it simple
because he can catch you

in a conversation,
and you'll be standing
there naked for so long
it'll get strange

listening to the guy
talk about his surgery,
all the while you're staring
at that scar straight down

his chest, and you're seeing
how skinny Ray is,
how he's kind of wobbly
on his feet, and his eyes

float off to the far
corners while he talks.
Meanwhile naked guys
move toward the showers, naked

guys move out of the showers,
while you're stuck there
naked, holding your towel,
and profoundly ready

for your own shower, but Ray's
deep into what the doctor
told him and what he said
to the doctor—you can stand

there for five, ten minutes
before Ray'll give you
an opening to get out
and finally into the water—

ah God, that hot water
does feel good on a body!
In there the muscle guys
soap down each little part

of their arms and legs,
butts and torsos—you almost
think that's what they live for,
getting into that shower

and letting the water whisper,
You're alive! You're alive!
I can appreciate that,
but my body doesn't argue

for me to stay in there
with them, my pate and paunch
and skinny chest making them
look younger and stronger.

I don't linger, that's what
I'm saying, that's my theme
song here, but when I'm out
and back at my locker, Ray's

still there, dressed now
and making a few concluding
remarks while he puts on his coat,
giving me his foxy smile,

as if to let me know
he knows I think he's ready
to start staying home now,
he's ready to follow

Al, the old fellow who had
to wear a diaper and used to have
that locker over there but whose
kids got him a place

in a retirement
community last year,
and now we don't see Al
any more, and Ray knows—

his hard little smile
tells me he knows—I don't
miss Al, and I'm not likely
to miss Ray either, but Ray

and I have a tacit
understanding of these
matters, we don't let
any of the big monsters

out of their cages, and so he
talks about the cold rain outside
while I nod and grunt
and step into my shorts.

Then Ray turns
as if he's seen
a pal he wants
to have a word

with, but there's nobody
behind him.
Then he turns back to me,
but now I've got my back

turned, and so there's this
awkward moment
when Ray's just standing there
with his coat on,

everything's been said
that could possibly be said,
naked men still
pass back and forth

and manly shouts
come from all parts
of the locker room,
but nobody

—and I witness this
out of the corner
of my eye, which is
officially looking elsewhere—

nobody really pays Ray
any mind at all. The guy
turns this way and that
and even slightly lifts his hand

before he sees whatever
it is that he sees
and he finally
goes out.

Brief Essay on Pain

A sudden radiance in my left palm—
maybe a small-caliber bullet-wound—
lasts about twenty-five seconds,
or until I'm just about to drop
the bag of groceries I'm carrying
and start whooping and violently
flapping my hand. Then it stops

and goes away. You're the only one
I've told this to—nothing happened,
no one saw, I didn't cry out, maybe
my imagination just thought my body
needed a jolt of martyrdom. Anyway
I get the groceries into the kitchen
and my hand looks perfectly normal.

I have friends who are gravely ill.
I'd be embarrassed to tell them all
my little throbs and stings. But death
has to start somewhere. The stroke
that slams you down into oblivion
could begin as the slightest tingle
in your left pinkie while you're sipping

your frappuccino in Barnes & Noble.
I think about Molly as a toddler,
putting her hand against the wood stove
at my parents' house and her expression
directed toward me as her witness
exactly when she realized how much hurt
had just entered her body. Bad God!—

to let such a thing happen to a child.
But of course that was nothing compared
to what thousands of children endure
every single day. There should be
a Painometer—a little dial on everybody's
forehead that shows how much you're feeling
in any given moment. Even then there'd be

these sudden spikes no one would see.
My palm episode, for instance, maybe set
a record for random, excruciating
temporary discomfort, and I had it all
completely to myself. I don't know
what that means. The New Testament
is basically a story about torture.

Deathlight

Each morning I wake up, a boy again,
but at night I trudge to bed, an old man.
I'm fifty-eight. Obituaries speak
to me now as poems did in my twenties.
"Light takes the tree," words that once named the pure
fact of beauty, I've learned to read as *Death
will turn all living matter into so
much energy.* Finite wattage. Shazam!
Suddenly I'll be starlight rocketing
through space toward another galaxy.
An average car lasts about twelve years,
a butterfly lives two days—when you think
about it, the human apparatus
is sturdier than it looks. Suicides
get thwarted by the body's insistence
on one more day of sunlight, one more spoon
full of oatmeal, or maybe just the hope
of a daughter's smile as she walks toward
the old failing thing. Did I tell you that
as a boy I was so afraid of the dark
I used to bribe my brother to keep me
company when I went to the bathroom
at night? But I think I'm slowly building
affection. Up on the mountain, the path
to Johnson Pond leads down through deepening
layers of darkness. Then it opens onto
silvery water with cool air rising
to your skin like death giving you a peck
on the cheek, so gently reminding you
of your true destination that you think,
Oh this is not bad, this is kind of nice.
What the obituaries never say,
though, is what keeps me reading them—in fact,
it's their lies ("after a courageous
battle . . . ," "peacefully passed . . . ," etc.)
that seem to keep the secret I'm after:
At the exact moment, could you tell if
she fell to darkness or burst into light?
But that's not it either. Oh, I don't know
what I want to know.

Remarkable Birdsong in Denton, Texas

1.

In a mean, cold rain,
after my worst meal
in thirty-five years,
I run under trees

where birds feast
on seeds or blossoms
that make them sing
as if they've flown

back to paradise
instead of migrating
to Texas. When I dash,
splashing, beneath that

canopy of birdsong,
I lose an entire
evening of self-
pity and complaint.

2.

Next day I learn
the grackles
are such a nuisance
the university

discourages them
with fireworks shot
into the very trees
where they sang me

through last night's
rain. I imagine
Roman candles
blasting them out,

the committee
deliberating
how to purge the God
damned things.

3.

Traveling, I become
one who's lost
a life and must
seek another.

Anyone I meet
makes a self
arise—hater,
lover, coward,

salesman, priest,
acne-faced boy
with a hard-on.
Tonight, before we lie

down to sleep,
we pray the little monks
will sing again
to help us rest.

4.

Home today! The poem
won't stand sixteen
repetitions of just two
words; therefore, I speak

of hurtling through clouds,
squeezed into the tightest
proximity of strangers,
and nevertheless not

dying the thousands
of moments death's
breath chills my neck—no
living creature

escapes a desperate
struggle: so sings
the one who flew away,
the one now winging home.

The Poem, The Snow, Jane Goodall, the Vase of Daffodils

1.

The poem was nothing
until I began wondering
what it is
about snow and a poem,

but that snow was something.
All day it wouldn't stop.
Soft, relentless, it meant
to white us out.

Hours, days, and months,
Jane Goodall sat quietly
beside her chimpanzees,
speaking only occasionally.

Morning sunlight on new snow;
indoors, on the table, this
vase of daffodils—the house's
heathen whispers *Alleluia.*

2.

Jane Goodall didn't want
to be a chimpanzee, and they
understood that.[1] But sometimes
for brief moments, she was.

Utterly irrational is how
you have to describe a vase
of daffodils except on the day
it makes perfect sense.

When it snows, write a poem.
Observe the white-caked limbs
of the apple tree. Yesterday
a chunk fell down my collar.

Often Jane Goodall spoke
a long while to a single chimpanzee.
She and the monkey understood it
wasn't going to speak back.

1. This you'd have to get from observing the seating arrangement. There's a bit of distance between them, as if Goodall has conveyed to the animals that she's really not after cozying up with them, stroking, them, petting them. Thus, they allow her to witness them, to sit in their presence—but only because they know that's all she wants.

3.

You don't want to read
a poem about poetry? Please
don't read this. I won't
know the difference.

Yellow, one of my favorite words,[2]
does no more justice to them
than does *intelligent* or *poignant*
to a chimpanzee's face.

No wonder
snow is so intent
on *whitening*
everything.

Jane Goodall's patience—
in her voice, her face, the way
she sat, even how she let
the baby chimp lick her arm.

2. Consider, for instance, that my grandfather, who worked for the New Jersey Zinc Company in the 20's, once decided that every one of a row of workers' houses should be painted yellow. Consider, for instance, that in Ben Shahn's *Spring, 1947,* the girl jumping rope far in the background wears a yellow dress. Consider, for instance, that the one shirt I have loved best of all I have ever owned was a yellow button-down Gant that I bought at Eljo's in Charlottesville for about $13.00.

4.

How to punish the ones
who can't stop themselves?
Make them never live
away from cut flowers.

In a city maybe Jane Goodall
turned into a hateful bitch.
To become the saint she was
she must have needed the chimps.

That morning of the deep snow
the warden permitted each a turn
walking out to the softball field
to make his own individual angel.

Actually, the vase is a crystal
beer mug.[3] Desirous of daffodils,
the poem nevertheless won't
tolerate certain kinds of lies.[4]

---

3. Vase, beer mug, whatever—it was Lindsey's hands that arranged them in it and set it on the table where it would catch the sun.

4. This, of course, is not true. You can put anything you want in a poem. My little story of the prisoners making snow angels, for instance.

5.

March 26th—the flowers' third day
in the house, third day of working
on the poem. The first layer
of snow arrived before Christmas.

Jane Goodall tells how poachers
kill the mother chimps to kidnap
and sell the babies. She gets quiet.
She looks down. She stays quiet.

The poem lives on my hard drive
and maybe—sort of—in my brain.
I could have a stroke.
My computer could crash.

In a court of poetry, daffodils
testify and so does snow.
Little matters as much
as Jane Goodall's long silence.

6.

A man and a woman begin
to laugh as they hit
a tennis ball back and forth.
They never say what's so funny.

Mid-phrase, a chamber group stops
playing and lapses into laughter.
Finally the cellist says,
"Okay, let's try that part again."

Depending on your sense of humor,
mood, and quality of imagination,
the above accounts are either
daffodils or snow. Die trying

for that intense connection—
Jane Goodall spent ten years
mostly sitting near
the creatures she loved.

The Penguin Sonatas

1. Myth

Maybe every penguin remembers
how it was to fly, though of course penguins
haven't for [plug in a big number] years.

Back then their wings were powerful engines,
not these ridiculous appendages
that show how foul God's sense of humor is.

Fact is, there was a moment many ages
ago, when it looked like God was about
to get His divine butt kicked—His rages

set the heavens on fire. "Those arrogant
penguins!" He'd shout and flame a galaxy
into oblivion. The ancient

penguins flew like F-110s, exactly
in unison and a million of them
at once, soaring up and only maxxing

out after they'd grazed God's toes and made Him
panic. They were sleek and sharp and cocky
and thought it was good that God imagine

being completely penguinized, okay
for Him to feel a little threatened. God
got furious one day when the whole sky

blackened with penguins executing these odd
maneuvers that suggested Satanic
influence. He'd had it!—He gave the nod

that shriveled their wings, and those birds dropped like
sacks of salt, spattering the continents.
The survivors came down in the arctic

zones, cushioned by deep banks of snow. Intense
desire for revenge motivates them now.
Small, slow, and clumsy—sure, they look harmless,

but they're evolving. Real funny fellow—
God. They'll get Him back, they don't care how.

2. Work Week

At dawn on Monday
I brew the vat of coffee
for my lovers. All day I serve them—
cream, sugar, each getting her special cup
and tiny engraved spoon. At night
I fall into bed,
exhausted,
alone.

On Tuesday I supervise the orchids.
Every week I explain to them why,
ultimately, they must release
their fragrance. They listen
quietly, bobbing
orchidaceously
on the breeze's current.
Sometime during the afternoon
one tells me that they have thought
it over and decided it is impossible.
"You would die," it whispers, "if we did."

On Wednesday I am an athlete.
My new jock strap and jog bra
make me feel unusually strong.
I acknowledge the applause
that greets me at breakfast,
but I refuse autographs to all
but one of my fans, a talented
child named Tina scheduled for
the electric chair next week.
I have my own personal squad
of cheerleaders, a hand-picked
group of teammates whose role

is to exchange leaping high-
fives with me when I score,
and an entourage of attractive
friends on whom I can depend to
be cheerful and lift my spirits
if I fall into low self-esteem.

I devote Thursday to silence. This is my hardest day.
Any little movement causes a rustling of bedcovers
or clothes, and if I clink a spoon against
my cereal dish, I must start the whole
morning over again. My dog greets
me at the bottom of the steps—
Don't bark! I convey to him
with just my eyes. *Don't
even wag your silly
tail!*

Fridays
are penguin-
appreciation days.
I take very small steps,
walk with my arms clamped rigidly
to my sides, and cast my eyes upward
in the direction of the Penguin Deity.
At the sushi restaurant I have my own table,
and a waitress wearing this very cool black and white kimono
uses chopsticks to stuff raw tuna down my throat.

Saturdays
I watch TV—
it's funny, all morning
I look forward to watching sports,
I've usually got a game I really want
to see, then I turn it on and find myself
completely enthralled by the weather channel,
thinking, man, this is a lot more interesting
than you'd think it would be, but the fact is
the only programs that give you any insight
at all into what it means to be
a human being are the animal
shows. Everything else
is for zombies.

Sundays I reserve for conversations with my Dead. My dad
and I like to talk about what his life would have been
like if he hadn't started smoking at the age
of seven. My mom and I go over each
of my old girlfriends and which one
would have made the best wife
for me. Aunt Inez and I
discuss whether she was
too crazy to love
anybody. Gran
and I
reminisce
about croquet
games the family
played those Sunday
afternoons when the slanting
sun coated the grass with buttery
light and the grown-ups drank mint juleps,
and Grandad explains how he didn't really hate
the old woman, it was just that he couldn't think
of any way to speak of the disaster his life had become.

3. The Penguin Sonatas

Certain phenomena—
say, for instance, the long-awaited arrival of the females
after their seasonal

feeding journey—
cause a grand clamor to arise from the coagulated
tribe of penguins,

a choral ululation
consisting of the thousand-fold croaks uttered skyward
from their beaks,

their tongues and throats—
actually that noise issues up out of the whole penguin body
as if its individual

life had to be
set forth and disclosed in a sort of biological prayer
to a deity

brooding over
whether or not the future should include such comically
desperate creatures.

This noise—the combined
autobiographies of approximately thirteen hundred
variously aged birds,

a group shriek,
as it were, the penguins' plea to be allowed to continue
their unspeakably

harsh existence—
provoked weeping from several Antarctic zoologists studying
the nesting habits

of Adélie penguins.
"It wasn't the noise—though in such cold that was quite
stirring," said one

scientist. "It was
what came afterward, as if the *silence* were transmitting
a response.

No member of our team
heard a sound, but with no understanding whatsoever, every
one of us felt

something conveyed
and perfectly understood by the penguins. Our tears froze
to our faces."

4. Free Time

Never not
without tasks
at home, I
nevertheless

get goof-off
occasions
while I work—
like washing

the dishes
as my break
from marking
manuscripts,

or raking
the back yard
in between
laundry loads,

or even
tidying
magazines
piled atop

the coffee
table while
deciding
how to teach

poetic
form to kids
who'd call it
oxymo-

ronic if
they loved words
instead of
whatever

it is they
do love that
makes them write
the drivel-

driven dog-
gerel they
hand in in
the name of

poetry.
Well, I see
I'm goofing
off here, I'm

supposed to
write about
idleness,
but I've lapsed

into shop
talk and job
bitchery,
butchering

poetry
even as
I complain
about kids

who write bad
poems. Forgive
me, my friends,
my brain turns

back to two
years old, too
immature
to keep track

of this week's
assignment—
like right now
I've freed up

some time here
on the couch—
laptop perched
on pillow

over crotch—
I've unclocked
the tick-tock
that sockets

my life like
stinky socks
on bare feet,
and, yes, I

could go on
like this way
beyond what
anyone

wants to read,
so okay
I'll try to
put a stop

to the poem—
endings are
when you make
time your boss

again, leave
the poem's time-
less chamber,
put your feet

(reeking toes
and all) back
on the grind-
ing globe, you've

got work to
do, I do,
too, and to
two ladies

like yourselves,
this may look
like hard work,
but in fact

it's easier
than running
the penguin
farm back home.

5. Put a Little Structure in It

You know those nature programs
where they show the salmon swimming back up
the same river at the same time every year
and the wildebeests making their mad dash across
a raging river to get to the spring grasslands?
The other night I saw my all-time favorite—
The male penguins take care of their one newly hatched
baby for many, many days, while the females go out
into the ocean, swimming freely and stuffing themselves with
fish. Each baby sort of sits
on its parent's feet and there's a sort of pouch
under there that protects the baby from predators
and the brutal weather. Anyway, the mothers
all come back at once to the big pack of stationary
males, each one of which has a baby more or less
tucked up underneath its ass, and this exchange
has to occur—the father penguin
has to pass the baby penguin
over to the mother penguin
because the father is starving and hasn't got any more
food to puke up into the baby's beak,
but the mother is so full of food
she can hardly waddle across the ice.
So each mother locates her mate with her baby
all cozy down there underneath its daddy,
and it just has to happen, it's nature's way, etc.—
the baby's got to go over
from the father to the mother,
and it has to happen quickly
because the baby can't be exposed to
the ice and the freezing wind.
                                But then the father
doesn't want to give it up, he's gotten used to how
things are, and so the female has to whack him on the beak
with her beak and use other persuasive tactics
to make him give it up.
                                He does, of course—
because otherwise there wouldn't be any penguins

anywhere on the planet for the nature investigators
to go out and film and splice and edit and add voice-over to and all
the other flim-flam bullshit
that results in these programs for citizens
like myself,
                    who transcend the limits
of our lives
in the blue trance
of our TVs night
after night.

6. Everyday Life at the Penguin Farm

We agree on a line from Shakespeare, or
Frost or Engels, we just can't remember
which, but it begins, "No greater error . . ."
Just those three words, not the who or the where.

We agree on a line of cocaine—we've
been drinking all night. You've begun to weave
through the crowd like a crazy woman. Eve,
when we get home, I swear I'm gonna leave.

We agree on a line we'll walk from here
to Wichita. The rule is wherever
the line takes us—sky scraper, nuclear
testing site, tar pit—we'll walk right through there.

We agree on a line of ants to stomp.
Oh, it's just the most fun, delightful romp
on a spring morning, each step death for ump-
teen ants. You hum "Circumstance and Pomp."

We agree on a line to tell your wife
and my husband. Don't say you don't know if
I'm worth it. Hand me my purse. See this knife?
If you think I'm cheap, examine your life.

We can't agree on the line they've taken.
Right now we don't have the slightest inkling
which way they went. Do you hear that tinkling?
It's their bells, I'll swear! Damn stupid penguins!

Curse Poem

Cursing God is good
for a thrill but stupid and useless.

Can't seem to curse death,
though it's claimed many I've loved.

Time, that ruthless bitch,
hides a bouquet of lilacs behind her back.

And sex? Curse sex,
and all I do is tell dirty jokes.

Curse cruelty and greed? War? Ignorance?
Sure, go ahead, shout at the mirror.

How about that well-known motherfucker, old age?
Yes, yes, yes! That's what I want to do,

but then just as I am about to hurl all the curses
I have within me, I see

I'm going to spit in the face
of my parents, Uncle Jack, Grandmama and Granddad.

Well, something needs to be cursed,
I'm certain of it, and I'm ready to do the job.

Damn you, pothole in the street!
Fuck you, skunk who sprayed my silly dog!

Go to hell, cucumber that rotted in my fridge!
And your mother's a whore,

little spider who scared me
yesterday in the shower!

Life on the Planet

A small spider appeared
atop the mirror, paused
and seemed to consider
crawling down the glass
across my lathered-up face.

Whenever I kill a spider,
I say, "Sorry, Grandmother."
When I don't, I see evidence
I possess a soul. Death
and redemption hovered.

If that thing crawled down
over my face, I'd swat it
into oblivion; if it stayed
at the edge, it could live
at least another day.

The mirror held the pink
arrangement of features,
I think of as me, and then
there was this minute blip
of protoplasm waving its legs.

Bones and flesh aside,
I am merely an archive
of acts and words—subtract
the good from the evil, I'd
probably come out a minus

or plus about the size
of my shaving companion,
who suddenly rappelled
out then clambered up
an invisible thread

to the ceiling where
I couldn't reach it—
as if to demonstrate
how little it cared
for me or my grandmother,

that righteous Methodist
lady who went so sweetly
to her death that nowadays
the whole family swears she
ascended straight to heaven.

Serpentine Wall

The summer I turned
twenty I met a girl
who liked just what
I liked, beer until
well after midnight,
then a stroll along
the winding wall Mr.
Jefferson contrived
to save bricks, our
destination unnamed
but known perfectly
well by both of us,
a bench in a pocket
of trees and shrubs
where we became Eve
and Adam, underwear
just got in the way,
and God didn't care
what we did as long
as we stopped short
of where our bodies
would take us, were
not our minds still
alert to the noises
and lights from out-
side the boundaries
of that garden wall.
THE TRUTH SHALL SET
YE FREE we saw each
night over the gate
to the University's
brick paths. Mind's
truth is one thing,
body's another, and
through these years
I've fallen farther
than I ever dreamed
I would, from happy
necking in a summer
garden, or any kind
of truth that set a
human being free for
more than about half
a heartbeat or less.

Circus

Surely I've seen one
so clearly do I hold
in mind the elephant
the clowns and lions

an almost naked lady
flying above my head
caught by the strong
man who swung upside

down merely to clasp
her breakable wrists
for thirteen seconds
before releasing her

into her triple flip
my mother and father
thrilled embarrassed
two country bumpkins

giving the circus to
their sons when it's
in town let there be
seals twirling balls

on their noses o let
there be a tightrope
walker a midget car
for the rowdy clowns

a mustachioed animal
trainer snapping his
whip forcing a tiger
to jump atop a horse

galloping in circles
then jumping through
a flaming hoop can I
have a big loud band

with trombones drums
and cornets a family
of smart chimpanzees
dressed up in shorts

ties dresses bonnets
can I please have my
brothers young again
our parents innocent

                                        of the future's dark
                                        cages or the animals
                                        suffering the maimed
                                        bodies of the clowns

                    and can we please be
                    charmed by the grand
                    master of ceremonies
                    who seemed so benign

in his power that we
knew the world would
go on astonishing us
long after we'd left

                    the big tent but now
                    that I think it over
                    I'm not sure we ever
                    got near a circus we

                                        probably just stared
                                        at a tattered poster
                                        in my family we were
                                        all good at dreaming

www.ingramcontent.com/pod-product-compliance
Lightning Source LLC
Chambersburg PA
CBHW060556100426
42742CB00013B/2588